Hands-On History

Colonial America

by Michael Gravois

New York • Toronto • London • Auckland • Sydney
Mexico City • New Delhi • Hong Kong • Buenos Aires

SCHOLASTIC
Teaching
Resources

Dedication

To my sister Stephanie

Cover design by Jason Robinson
Interior design by Michael Gravois
Interior illustrations by Jim Palmer and Mona Mark

ISBN 0-439-58716-6

Copyright © 2003 by Michael Gravois. All rights reserved.

Printed in the U.S.A.

3 4 5 6 7 8 9 10   40   10 09 08 07 06 05 04

Table of Contents

Introduction

As a middle-school teacher, I was always looking for ways to keep students interested and enthusiastic about learning. I developed activities and projects that helped me teach the required curriculum and also made my lessons fun, hands-on, diverse, and challenging.

I used an interactive-project approach with my fifth-grade students, and I can't stress enough how much they enjoyed it. Throughout each unit I had my students keep the activity sheets and projects in a pocket folder, so they could assemble a student-made textbook on the subject we were studying. They used these textbooks as a study guide for the final test. I was amazed at the higher-level thinking that took place in class discussions and by the degree of knowledge the students had acquired by the end of each unit. Parents even commented on the unique way the information was presented and how easy it was for their children to study for the final test. After seeing my students' success, I decided to put my ideas on paper. *Hands-On History: Colonial America* is a compilation of the activities I used to teach Colonial America.

For each activity and project, I've included detailed instructions. Many of the activities incorporate language arts and critical thinking skills such as differentiating fact and opinion, comparing and contrasting, the 5 Ws, cause and effect, writing a letter, brainstorming, and sequencing.

I hope your students enjoy these projects as much as mine did.

How to Use This Book

Supplies

At the beginning of the school year, ask students to bring in the materials needed to create projects throughout the year. Also arrange the classroom desks into clusters, each with a bin to hold pens, markers, glue sticks, scissors, and other needed supplies. This enables students to share the materials. You should have each of your students bring in the following supplies:

- a roll of tape
- several glue sticks
- a good pair of scissors
- a packet of colored pencils
- a packet of thin, colored markers
- a project folder (pocket-type) to hold papers and other materials related to the projects

Maximizing Learning

Because students have different learning styles, you may want to first orally summarize the information you will be covering that day. Then you can read the related section in the textbook or trade book. Finally, have students complete the activity. This not only exposes visual, aural, and artistic learners to the information through their strongest learning style, but it also allows all students to review the same information several times.

Melting Pot Bulletin Board

Materials: copies of pages 27–28, colored markers, scissors, glue sticks, colored construction paper (for title)

North America has always been a land of great diversity and economic opportunity. Its sheer size not only offered a variety of climatic and geographic differences, but provided abundant resources as well. As word spread of these resources and more and more people sought to inhabit this land, each group brought with them their own beliefs and culture to contribute to the large melting pot that is America. To illustrate the diversity that began in early America, start by looking at the diversity in your own classroom.

CREATING THE BULLETIN BOARD

Have each student interview family members and then write a two-paragraph history of their family. You may wish to have them use the reproducible graphic organizer on page 28 to organize their ideas. Students should write about when their ancestors first came to America, why they came, and who they were. Ask them to find out as much about their family history as possible. They can then read these short family biographies to the class.

After completing the family histories, give each student a copy of the reproducible "melting pot" silhouette on page 27. Ask them to color the pot and cut it out. Staple each of the pots to the bulletin board, leaving the top open. Have students insert their family biographies into their pot on the board. Finally, add a title made out of construction paper, such as "The American Melting Pot."

CREATING THE TITLE PAGE

At the end of the unit, the family biographies created for the bulletin board can serve as the title page for the student-made textbook.

1. Give each student another copy of the Colonial America melting pot reproducible from page 27 and an additional blank sheet of paper.
2. Ask students to decorate the melting pot.
3. Have them cut the dotted line that runs across the top of the pot and glue just the perimeter of this page to the blank one behind it.
4. Fold the family biography and insert it into the melting pot.

Colonial America Vocabulary Bulletin Board

Materials: copies of page 29, brown paper for background,
green construction paper for trees, colored markers

At the beginning of your Colonial America unit, set up a vocabulary bulletin board, which students add to as the unit unfolds. First, cover the bulletin board with brown paper to look like land, and add a title banner that says "Colonial America Vocabulary." Have each student create two fir trees for the scene using green construction paper.

Students take turns writing each new vocabulary word and its definition on a log cabin from the reproducible on page 29. Students decorate the log cabins as they choose. Keep a supply of these "vocabulary log cabins" handy for students to use as new words come up during the unit. See the list below and on page 7 for some possible vocabulary words and their definitions.

VARIATION

As an alternative to the bulletin board idea, have each student assemble a "Colonial America Dictionary," which can be bound into a student-created textbook at the end of the unit. To do this, reduce the size of the template so that six log cabins fit on each page.

Word List

cash crop: a crop that is grown to sell for money

charter: an official document issued by a ruler giving someone the right to establish a colony on land claimed by the ruler

common: a large, grassy area in the center of New England towns where animals often grazed

debtor: a person who owes money

Huguenots: French Protestants who fled from France to escape persecution; many settled in the Carolinas

Word List (continued)

indentured servant: a person who sold his or her services for a fixed period of time in exchange for passage to America

indigo: a plant that is used to produce a blue dye

joint-stock company: a company in which many people share ownership, ensuring that no one person risks all of his or her money

meeting house: a central building in early New England villages where town meetings and church services were held

overseer: a person hired to supervise a plantation and its slaves

Pilgrim: a person who travels to a foreign land for religious reasons

proprietor: an owner

Puritans: members of the Church of England who wanted to "purify" the church and focus on worshipping God. They settled the colony of Massachusetts.

Quakers: a peace-loving religious group that started in England and settled in Pennsylvania

Separatist: a person who separated from the Church of England because of religious disagreements

stock: a share in a company

Roanoke Island Q & A Datadisk

Materials: copies of page 30, glue sticks, scissors, metal brads, oaktag or construction paper

One of the great mysteries from America's past concerns the disappearance of the Roanoke Island colonists. After the class reads about and discusses the events leading up to this puzzling event, ask students to follow the directions on page 8 to create a datadisk recording their findings.

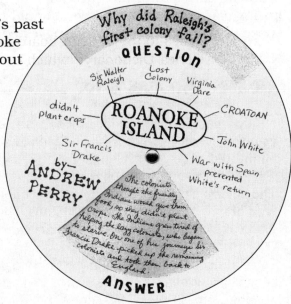

CREATING THE DATADISK

1. Pass out a copy of the datadisk from page 30 and two pieces of oaktag (or construction paper) to each student.
2. Instruct students to follow the directions on the datadisk template.
3. Have students complete the "Roanoke Island" word web and write questions and answers in the Q and A spaces, following the steps desribed below.

BRAINSTORMING

Draw a circle on the board and write "Roanoke Island" inside the circle. Ask students to tell you the name of a person associated with the Roanoke colony. Write the name on the board and draw a line from the circle to the person's name. On the cover of their datadisks, students should write the person's name. Then have them draw a line from the title "Roanoke Island" to the person's name. Tell them to brainstorm as many people, places, and things associated with the Roanoke colony as possible. They should draw a line from the title to each word or phrase. Discuss the ideas as a class. Some suggested words and phrases are included in the word web to the right.

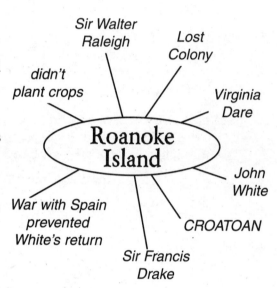

FINISHING THE DATADISK

Have students write the following suggested questions in the "Question" space of their datadisk, rotating the disk one-third revolution for each one.

Question 1: Who was Sir Walter Raleigh?
Question 2: Why did Raleigh's first colony fail?
Question 3: What happened to the second colony?

Students can answer the questions for homework or by working with a partner during class time. Each answer should be written in the corresponding "Answer" space beneath each question. Suggested answers appear below.

Suggested Answers for Datadisk

1. Raleigh was a wealthy friend of the Queen of England, who gave him permission to start a colony in North America. Twice he tried to start a colony in North Carolina, but both times he failed.

2. The colonists did not plant enough crops to support the colony. The Indians nearby grew tired of providing the colonists with food. The colonists began to starve and a ship from England picked up the surviving colonists.

3. England became involved in a war with Spain and sent no ships to check the colony for three years. When a ship finally arrived, there was no sign of life in the colony. The only clue was the word "CROATOAN" carved into a tree.

Jamestown Study Guide

Materials: copier paper, copies of page 31, scissors, tape

After learning about Jamestown, ask students to complete the following activities and construct a fold-out study guide filled with information relating to the first successful English colony in North America.

BRAINSTORMING

Pass out a sheet of blank white paper to each student. On the top half of this page, have students create a brainstorming web like the one shown below (some possible ideas are included). Students can work individually or in pairs to list people, places, and events that relate to Jamestown.

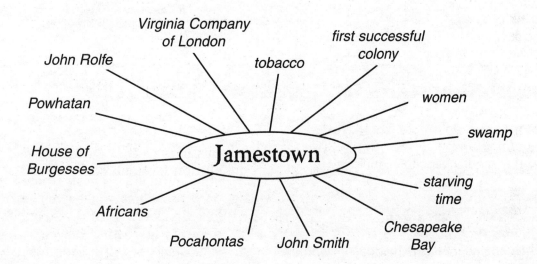

COMPLETING THE STUDY GUIDE

1. Pass out copies of page 31 to students.
2. Discuss the different problems the colonists faced and guide students to fill in the blanks.
3. Discuss the reasons why Jamestown grew and prospered, again filling in the blanks.
4. After they have completed the panels, have students cut them out and tape one edge of each to the bottom of the paper used for the brainstorming web. See the example at the top of page 10.

COMPLETING THE INSIDE PANELS

1. After they have attached the panels, ask students to open them and write the following names across the tops of the four inside panels: Virginia Company of London, John Smith, Pocahontas, John Rolfe.

2. Below each name, have students write three complete sentences describing the contribution each made to the success of the Jamestown colony.

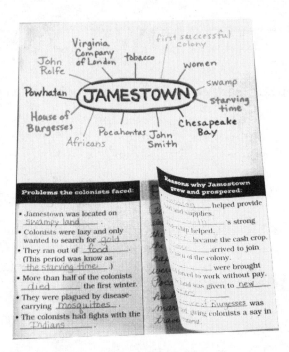

Suggested Answers for Jamestown Study Guide

Problems the Colonists Faced:
swampy land; gold; food; The Starving Time; died; mosquitoes; Indians

Reasons Why Jamestown Grew and Prospered:
Powhatan; John Smith; tobacco; women; Africans; new settlers; House of Burgesses

Virginia Company of London:
After Sir Walter Raleigh lost much of his money trying to establish a colony, people in England began forming joint-stock companies to invest in colonies. In such a company, many people share the risk and the benefit, so no one person is in danger of losing everything. The Virginia Company of London was a joint-stock company that started the colony of Jamestown.

John Smith:
Because the Virginia Company insisted that the colonists share the food that they grew, few of the colonists planted crops. Many spent their time searching for gold. John Smith took charge and put an end to laziness by declaring that "He that will not work, shall not eat." His strong leadership helped the colony to survive.

Pocahontas:
She was the eleven-year-old daughter of the Powhatan chief. When the Powhatan Indians captured John Smith and were going to kill him, Pocahontas pleaded for his life. Years later, she married John Rolfe and traveled to England.

John Rolfe:
John Rolfe introduced tobacco to Jamestown. Tobacco became a cash crop and brought a lot of money to the colonists. Rolfe also formed an alliance with the Powhatan Indians by marrying Pocahontas.

Accordion Book of Plymouth

Materials: copier paper (3 sheets per student), scissors, tape, colored markers

After learning about Plymouth Colony, have students create a pocket page that features information from their studies. (This pocket page will hold their accordion book of Plymouth Colony.)

CREATING THE POCKET PAGE

Give each student two sheets of copier paper and have them fold one in half widthwise. Next, have them insert the unfolded sheet into the folded sheet. Finally, have them tape the left and right edges of the folded sheet.

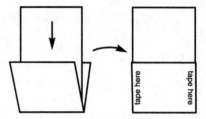

BRAINSTORMING

On the top half of the page, above the pocket, have students create a brainstorming web of Plymouth. They can work individually or in pairs to list people, places, and events that relate to Plymouth. Review the answers as a class, creating a large web on the board and filling in students' ideas. Some suggested answers are shown in the web to the right.

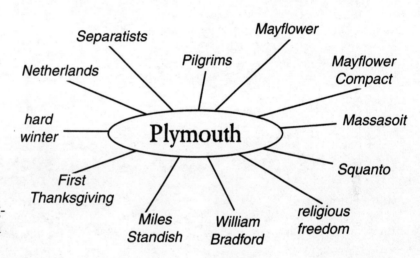

CREATING THE ACCORDION BOOK

Pass out another sheet of copier paper to students for creating the accordion book of Plymouth Colony. Guide students to follow the directions below.

1. Cut the paper vertically up the center.
2. Tape the two lengths together, end to end.
3. Fold the paper accordion-style so that there are six panels.
4. On the top panel write "(your name)'s Accordion Book of Plymouth Colony" using creative lettering. Draw a related picture on the cover.
5. Open up the accordion book to reveal the six blank panels. Write each of the following words at the top of a panel, in this sequence: Netherlands, Plymouth, Mayflower Compact, First Winter, Squanto, First Thanksgiving.
6. Fill in each panel by writing several sentences describing the topic and creating an illustration for each. (Suggested responses are found on page 12.)

Students can begin this activity in class and finish it for homework. When they have completed their accordion books, have students insert them into their pocket pages.

Suggested Answers for Accordion Book

Netherlands:
A group of people did not agree with the teachings of the Church of England, so they left England and moved to the Netherlands.

Plymouth:
Fearing that their children were becoming "too Dutch," the Separatists left the Netherlands and headed for Virginia. A storm blew them off course and they landed on Cape Cod, where they established Plymouth Colony.

Mayflower Compact:
Before setting foot on land, the Pilgrims drew up a set of laws that each person agreed to follow. This document was called the Mayflower Compact.

First Winter:
Because the Pilgrims arrived in the fall, they were unprepared for the harsh winter ahead. More than half the people died during that first winter.

Squanto:
The next spring, an Indian named Squanto taught the Pilgrims how to hunt and fish— skills necessary for their survival. He also showed them how to plant crops and how to use fish to fertilize the soil.

First Thanksgiving:
In the fall, the Pilgrims and the Indians held a large feast to celebrate their friendship and to give thanks for the good harvest.

Comparing the Colonies

Materials: copies of page 32

Ask students to review the three interactive study guides that they have created for the colonies of Roanoke, Jamestown, and Plymouth. Then pass out copies of the Comparing the Colonies reproducible on page 32. Students can complete the activity for homework, or you can use it as a quiz. The completed and corrected activity can be added to students' self-made textbooks at the end of the unit.

Answers

1. P	6. P	11. R	16. J, P
2. J	7. J	12. R	17. J
3. R	8. P	13. P	18. P
4. J	9. J	14. J	19. P
5. R	10. R, J, P	15. J	20. R

Map of the Thirteen Colonies

Materials: copies of page 33, colored markers

Pass out a copy of the map of the thirteen colonies on page 33. Have students select three colors and color in the boxes for the key indicating the New England Colonies, the Middle Colonies, and the Southern Colonies. As they learn about each colony in the next three activities, ask students to write the colony's name under the correct heading, use the appropriate color to outline the colony on the map, and label the colony with the postal abbreviation of the current state. Students should keep this map in their project folder so it is easily accessible throughout the unit. It can be added to their self-made textbooks when they complete the unit.

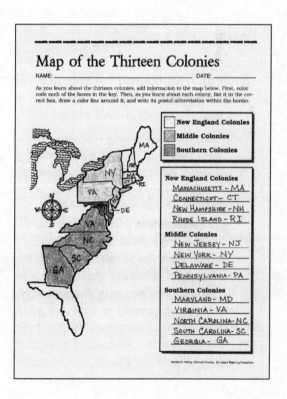

13

Four-Fold Book of the New England Colonies

Materials: copies of page 34, scissors, colored markers

As students learn about the New England colonies, they should add the information to the map as described on page 13.

CREATING THE FOUR-FOLD BOOK

Students will create a four-fold book in which they describe the four colonies of New England and explain the concept of the triangular trade.

1. Pass out copies of page 34. If your copier accepts paper larger than 8½" x 11", enlarge the scale of the four-fold book to give students more room to write.
2. Have students cut out the cross shape and fold the four flaps on the dotted lines.
3. On the blank side of each folded flap, instruct students to write the names of the four New England colonies. Then ask them to write a few sentences about the founding of each colony.
4. After studying the New England colonies, have students fill in the blanks on the graphic by listing the correct trade items that moved through each leg of the triangle. Then ask them to write a brief paragraph describing how this trade system worked.

Suggested Answers for Four-Fold Book

NEW ENGLAND COLONIES—

Massachusetts:
Like the Pilgrims before them, the Puritans were unhappy with the teachings of the Church of England. Led by John Winthrop, they left England and sailed to North America in 1630. They started the Massachusetts Bay Colony. The first settlement was Boston.

Rhode Island:
Roger Williams and Anne Hutchinson both disagreed with Puritan leaders in Boston. They fled that colony and started their own settlements in Providence and Portsmouth, Rhode Island.

Connecticut:
Thomas Hooker also left Massachusetts, because he believed that each church should be independent. In 1636, he founded the colony of Connecticut with about a hundred followers.

(continued on page 15)

Suggested Answers for Four-Fold Book (Continued)

New Hampshire:
In the late 1630s, colonists who were looking for more farmland and good places to fish settled in the area that became the colony of New Hampshire.

TRIANGULAR TRADE SYSTEM—

New England:
dropped off molasses; picked up rum

Africa:
dropped off rum; picked up slaves

West Indies:
dropped off slaves; picked up molasses

THE TRIANGULAR TRADE—
The triangular trade got its name because trade ships stopped in three different ports, dropping off and picking up cargo. Molasses was taken from the West Indies to New England, where it was traded for rum. The rum was taken to Africa, where the merchants traded it for enslaved people. The slaves were taken to the West Indies where they were sold to work on the sugar plantations. The sugar was used to make molasses.

Mini-Books of the Middle Colonies

Materials: directions on page 17, copier paper, scissors, colored markers

As students learn about the Middle Colonies, they should add the information to the map as described on page 13.

CREATING THE MINI-BOOKS

In this activity, students will make two mini-books: one focusing on the New York colony, and the other focusing on the remaining three Middle Colonies—Pennsylvania, New Jersey, and Delaware.

1. Ask students to follow the directions on page 17 to create two mini-books each. You may want to photocopy the directions on the top half of page 17 to distribute to students, or read them aloud to give students a chance to practice their listening skills.

2. On the cover of the first mini-book, have them write the title "My Mini-Book of the New York Colony" using creative lettering and draw a related picture.

3. Have students title the three double-page spreads "Henry Hudson and New Netherlands," "Peter Stuyvesant and New Amsterdam," and "The English and New York." Then have them write a few sentences about each topic and draw a related picture.

4. On the cover of the second mini-book, ask students to write the title "My Mini-Book of the Middle Colonies" in creative lettering and draw a related picture.
5. On the three double-page spreads, have students write the titles "Pennsylvania," "New Jersey," and "Delaware." Then students should write a few sentences about each colony and draw a related picture.

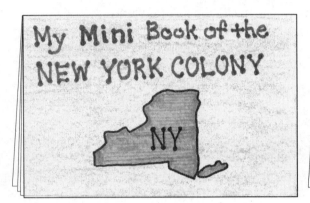

Suggested Answers for Mini-Books

NEW YORK COLONY MINI-BOOK—

Henry Hudson and New Netherlands:
In 1609, Henry Hudson tried to find the Northwest Passage to Asia for the Dutch. Sailing on the ship the *Half Moon*, he explored along the Hudson River and named the area New Netherlands.

Peter Stuyvesant and New Amsterdam:
The Dutch bought the island of Manhattan and named it New Amsterdam. They appointed Peter Stuyvesant the first governor. Stuyvesant was a very strict leader and quite unpopular with the people of the colony.

The English and New York:
In 1664, four English warships sailed into New Amsterdam harbor and demanded the Dutch surrender. Stuyvesant wanted to fight, but the colonists did not, and they surrendered without a shot being fired. The English king gave the colony to his brother, the Duke of York, and the settlement was renamed New York.

MIDDLE COLONIES MINI-BOOK—

Pennsylvania:
King Charles II of England gave a large area of land to William Penn to settle a debt with Penn's father. Penn, a Quaker, named the colony after his father. Many Quakers settled there, but people from all religions were welcome. The first settlement was Philadelphia.

New Jersey:
The Duke of York gave a large part of New York to two of his friends, Lord John Berkeley and Sir George Cartaret. They renamed the area New Jersey. In order to attract settlers, they allowed freedom of religion and sold land cheaply to settlers.

Delaware:
William Penn asked the king for more land and was given Delaware. Penn paid the Indians for this land, and the colonists and Indians lived in peace in this colony for many years.

Directions for Creating the Mini-Books

1. Fold a sheet of paper in half widthwise.

2. Fold it in half again in the same direction.

3. Fold this long, narrow strip in half in the opposite direction.

4. Open up the paper to the Step 2 position, and cut halfway down the vertical fold.

5. Open the paper up and turn it horizontally. There should be a hole in the center of the paper where you've made the cut.

6. Fold the paper in half lengthwise.

7. Push in on the ends of the paper so the slit opens up. Push until the center panels meet.

8. Fold the four pages into a mini-book and crease the edges.

Matchbooks of the Southern Colonies

Materials: copies of page 35, copier paper, scissors, tape, glue sticks, colored markers

As students learn about the Southern Colonies, they should add the information to the map as described on page 13.

CREATING THE MATCHBOOKS

First, students will create four small matchbooks, one for each of the Southern Colonies. After they complete the matchbooks, they will create a fold-out guide to the Southern Colonies.

1. Pass out copies of the matchbook templates on page 35.
2. Have students cut out the matchbooks and fold them on the dotted lines so that the colony name is facing up.
3. On the cover of each matchbook, ask students to draw a picture or icon related to each colony. (For example, they could draw an icon of a wrapped present for Maryland as a reminder that the colony was a gift to Lord Baltimore.)

4. Have students write a few sentences inside each matchbook about the person who founded the colony and the reason it was founded.

Virginia

The Carolinas

Georgia

CREATING A FOLD-OUT GUIDE

After completing the matchbooks of the four colonies, students can continue their study of the Southern Colonies by creating a fold-out guide.

1. Give students copies of pages 36 and 37. Ask them to cut along the dotted line on page 37. Then have students place the printed sides of the two pages facing each other so that the right edge of page 36 is next to the left edge of page 37. Have them tape these edges together so that the pages open to form a spread, as shown below.
2. Ask students to complete the activity sheet comparing slaves and indentured servants. This can be done in class or as homework.
3. Then have them turn to the other page, "Worlds Apart." In the Venn diagram, students should compare and contrast life on a plantation and life in the backcountry. You may wish to do this together as a class or assign it for homework.
4. Have students close the pages so that the back of the "Worlds Apart" template is on top and becomes the "cover page." The bottom page is wider than the top page, which allows students to bind the fold-out guide into a student-made, interactive notebook at the end of the unit. See page 26 for binding instructions.
5. Ask students to write the title "My Matchbooks of the Southern Colonies" in creative lettering across the top of this cover page.
6. Instruct students to attach the four matchbooks to the cover with a glue stick.

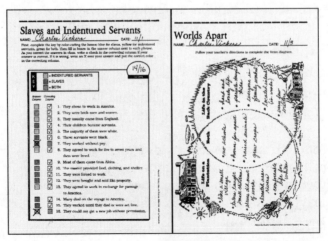

Suggested Answers for Matchbooks

Virginia:

The Virginia Company of London established the settlement of Jamestown. This settlement expanded to become the Virginia colony.

Maryland:

King Charles I gave George Calvert (Lord Baltimore) this land as a gift. Calvert named it after the queen. He wanted to create a colony for Roman Catholics, who were treated poorly in England. Calvert soon died, but his son established the colony.

North and South Carolina:

King Charles gave eight men, called proprietors, a charter to start a colony they named Carolina, in honor of the king. The two major settlements in this colony were far apart, so the proprietors split it into two colonies.

Georgia:

King George II was concerned that the Spanish would move north from Florida and threaten the English colonies; so he gave James Oglethorpe permission to create the colony of Georgia. Oglethorpe took many debtors from English prisons to settle the colony.

Answers for Slaves and Indentured Servants

1. indentured servants
2. both
3. indentured servants
4. slaves
5. indentured servants
6. slaves
7. both
8. indentured servants
9. slaves
10. both
11. slaves
12. slaves
13. indentured servants
14. slaves
15. slaves
16. both

Suggested Answers for Worlds Apart

Life on a Plantation
- like a small village
- tutors taught small children
- slaves did most of work
- located near rivers
- comfortable life for whites

Both
- no schools
- homes far apart
- raised animals
- grew crops

Life in the Back Country
- hard and lonely life
- parents taught kids
- everyone in family worked
- located inland (in woods)
- very few visitors

Circlebooks of Colonial Contrasts

Materials: copies of pages 38–40 on colored paper, white copier paper, scissors, glue sticks

This activity serves as an overall review of the ways in which the three groups of colonies differed from each other.

1. Copy each of the three circlebook templates onto colored paper (e.g. New England Colonies on blue, Middle Colonies on red, and Southern Colonies on yellow). Alternately, you can have students color-code the circles with colored markers.
2. Hand out the three colored sheets and one blank white sheet to each student. Have students write "Colonial Contrasts" in creative lettering across the top of the blank sheet.
3. Have students cut out the 12 circles and fold them vertically along the dotted lines.
4. Have students use a glue stick to attach the right half of a New England Colonies circle to the left half of a Middle Colonies circle (figure 1), and then attach the right half of the Middle Colonies circle to the left half of the Southern Colonies circle (figure 2).
5. Instruct students to glue the backs of the New England and Southern circles to the blank title page, and repeat the process for the remaining three sets of circles. Students will then have four circlebooks glued together, each containing one panel for each colony and one title page.
6. Above each of the circlebooks, ask students to write the following headings: Geographical, Economic, Educational, Political. (See the example above.)
7. As a class, discuss how the three groups of colonies differed in these four areas. List the answers on the chalkboard and have students write the answers on the corresponding circlebook pages. (Note: Consider having students write on the circles before they construct the circlebooks.) Suggested answers appear on page 21.

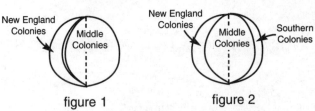

figure 1   figure 2

Class Quilt of Colonial America

Materials: copies of page 41, scissors, colored markers, tape

Quilting was an important part of life in Colonial America. Not only were quilts necessary for warmth in the harsh winters, but they provided an ideal social outlet for the colonists. They held quilting bees: a large group of people, usually women, would gather around a large table to make a quilt, tell stories, and teach the young girls quilting skills. By working together, they could finish the quilts much more quickly than if they quilted them individually; plus, it was more fun to work together.

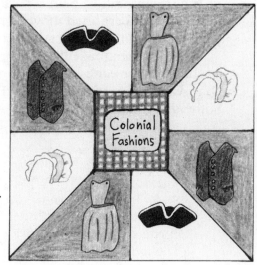

21

CREATING THE CLASS QUILT

1. Provide each student with a research topic on Colonial America (see suggestions below). Ask them to learn more about their topic by reading texts and trade books and by exploring the Internet.
2. Hand each student a copy of the quilt template from page 41. You may wish to share color pictures of colonial quilts with students before they begin the project. In the center of the template, they should write the name of their topic, using creative lettering.
3. In the eight sections surrounding the center, ask students to draw pictures or designs that relate to their research topic. Suggest that students make their designs in repeating or alternating patterns. For example, a student researching the colony of Georgia might make a pattern of cotton bolls.
4. When students have finished designing their quilt panels, have them cut out the panels and give a short oral report about their topic.
5. Then place all of the panels next to each other, face down, and tape them together to form a large quilt.
6. Hang the quilt on the wall or bulletin board under the title "Our Class Quilt of Colonial America."

SUGGESTED RESEARCH TOPICS

Colonial Williamsburg	Pocahontas
Salem Witch Trials	Native Americans
Mayflower	Colonial Fashions
First Thanksgiving	Life on a Plantation
Jobs in Colonial America	Slave Trade and Middle Passage
Colonial American Games	Education in Colonial America
Economy of Colonial America	Famous American Colonists

EXTENSION ACTIVITY

You may wish to incorporate creative dramatics and movement into the curriculum by having students "interpret" a quilt design. Divide your class into four or five groups and give each group a color photograph of a quilt design. Try to find designs that vary in color, symmetry, movement, and pattern. Give students about ten minutes to look at the design and to plan a performance that makes the quilt come alive through simple, choreographed movements. The movements should convey whether the pattern is light or dark, symmetrical or asymmetrical, and simple or complex.

You will be amazed at the creative solutions your students will find for this problem. After each presentation, ask the other students what they think the quilt that was performed looks like. Show the quilt to the class after they have made some guesses.

Readers Theater

Anne Hutchinson: An Outspoken Woman

Materials: copies of *Anne Hutchinson: An Outspoken Woman* (pages 42–48)

Reading plays aloud can provide students with opportunities to make connections between history and their own lives. Taking on a role, even for a short time, allows learners to become part of the story of our history, to become emotionally involved in the stories of other people, and to explore choices and lives foreign from their own.

Give each student a copy of the play *Anne Hutchinson: An Outspoken Woman* by Sarah J. Glasscock, and have your class read it aloud. Consider having your class perform the play for other classes or having them turn it into a radio play, complete with sound effects and music. You might even invite a local professional actor to speak with the class about the nature of acting and good stage techniques.

After your class reads the play, you may wish to use the following activities to extend students' understanding of Anne Hutchinson and Colonial America in general.

DIFFERENT VOICES IN THE COMMUNITY

John Winthrop hoped to set up a model community in America where Puritans would be free to worship. As Anne Hutchinson found out, the Massachusetts Bay Colony could be as oppressive as the monarchy in England. What do students think about the decision to banish Anne Hutchinson from the colony? How do we as Americans deal with different voices within our communities today? Ask students to present specific examples of opposing voices in their neighborhood, city or town, state, and nation. Discuss how the two (or more) sides in each example can forge a compromise.

A PRICE TO PAY

Anne Hutchinson's family accepted her banishment as their own. Ask your students how they would have felt if they were part of the Hutchinson family. Would they have encouraged Anne to speak out, or would they have urged her to keep silent? Was being kicked out of the colony too high a price to pay for supporting religious freedom?

A DAY IN THE MASSACHUSETTS BAY COLONY

The Massachusetts Bay Colony was founded over 300 years ago. The way people lived has changed considerably since then. Assign the task of finding out what life was like in the colony. Ask students to consider some of these topics: What did people wear? What did they eat? What kinds of games did children play? What holidays did the Puritans honor, and how did they celebrate? Encourage a diversity of presentations, such as writing a diary entry that details a man's, woman's, or child's typical day, or try celebrating a Puritan holiday in class.

Colonial America Study Guide

Create a wonderful study guide for your students by having them compile all of their mini-books, activities, and projects into an interactive Colonial America "textbook." Over the course of the unit, ask students to save all of their papers and projects in a pocket folder. At the end of the unit, use a binding machine to put them all together. If you don't have access to one, use a three-hole punch and yarn. On the next three pages you'll find suggestions for compiling each page.

Materials: all of the projects students have created, 8½" x 11" paper, binding machine (if available) or hole punch with yarn

COVER

When binding the textbooks, add a page of heavy stock to the front and back. Students can use creative lettering to add a title, and then draw a total of ten icons on the front and back covers. The icons can represent any ten things the student learned over the course of the unit. Have students number the icons, and then, on the inside front cover, write a complete sentence describing the significance of each icon.

PAGE 1

The MELTING POT pocket-page that holds each student's family history can act as the title page.

PAGE 2

Students can create a pocket-page to hold their ROANOKE ISLAND Q & A DATADISK. Create the pocket by folding a piece of 8½" x 11" paper in half horizontally, slipping another sheet of paper into the fold, and taping the sides. Encourage students to add a title and decorate the page.

PAGE 3

Include the JAMESTOWN STUDY GUIDE as page 3.

PAGE 4

Students can glue their ACCORDION BOOK OF PLYMOUTH onto a sheet of paper, which can be bound into their interactive text-books as page 4. Encourage students to add a title to the page.

PAGE 5

Use the COMPARING THE COLONIES activity sheet as page 5.

PAGE 6

The MAP OF THE THIRTEEN COLONIES becomes page 6 of the interactive textbook.

PAGE 7

Students can glue their FOUR-FOLD BOOK OF THE NEW ENGLAND COLONIES onto a sheet of paper, which can be bound in as page 7.

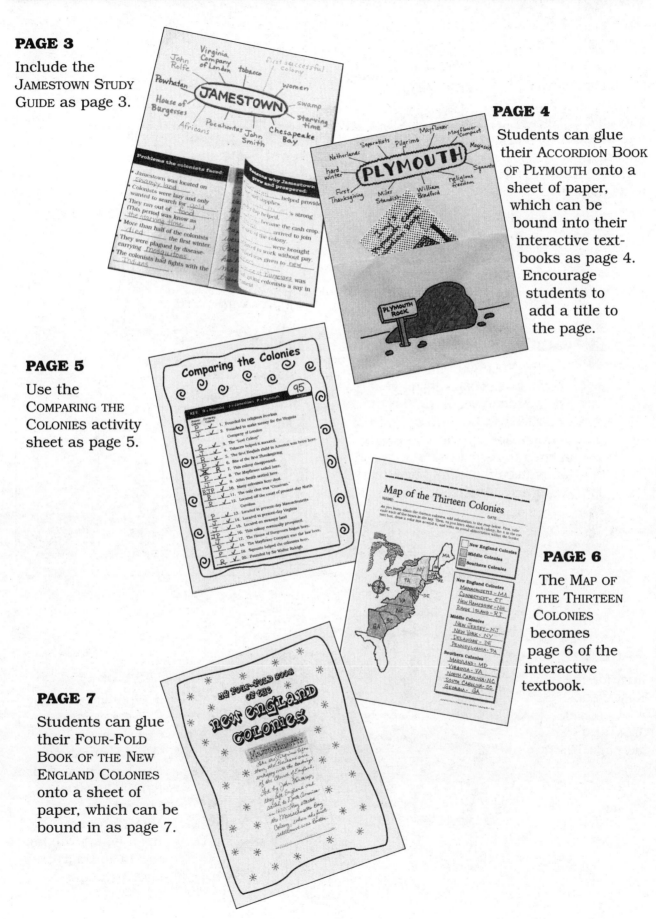

PAGE 8

Students can glue the backs of their MINI-BOOKS OF THE MIDDLE COLONIES to a sheet of paper, which can be bound in as page 8.

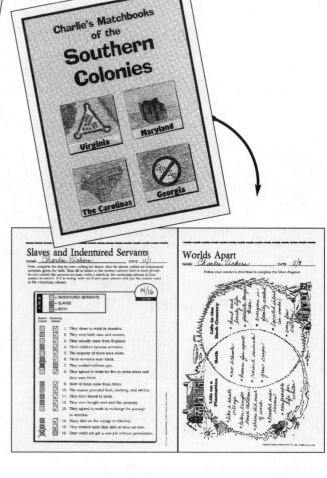

PAGE 9

Use the FOLD-OUT GUIDES OF THE SOUTHERN COLONIES for page 9. The MATCHBOOKS OF THE SOUTHERN COLONIES will be on top, and the double-page spread can be opened to reveal the SLAVES AND INDENTURED SERVANTS and WORLDS APART activity sheets.

PAGE 10

Include the CIRCLEBOOKS OF COLONIAL CONTRASTS as page 10.

PAGE 11

Finally, take the quilt squares down from the bulletin board, and have students glue their CLASS QUILT OF COLONIAL AMERICA squares to a sheet of paper, which will be page 11 in their interactive textbooks.

Colonial America

How my family became a part of America's melting pot.

Melting Pot Graphic Organizer

Complete this graphic organizer with your parents, grandparents, or other family members.

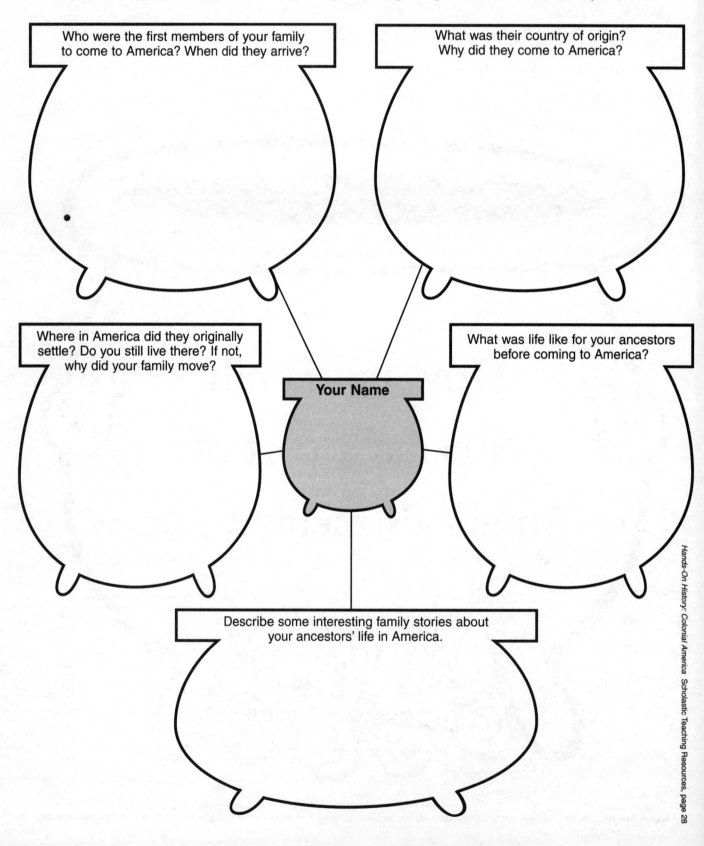

Who were the first members of your family to come to America? When did they arrive?

What was their country of origin? Why did they come to America?

Where in America did they originally settle? Do you still live there? If not, why did your family move?

Your Name

What was life like for your ancestors before coming to America?

Describe some interesting family stories about your ancestors' life in America.

Vocabulary Log Cabins

word:

_____

definition:

_____

_____

_____

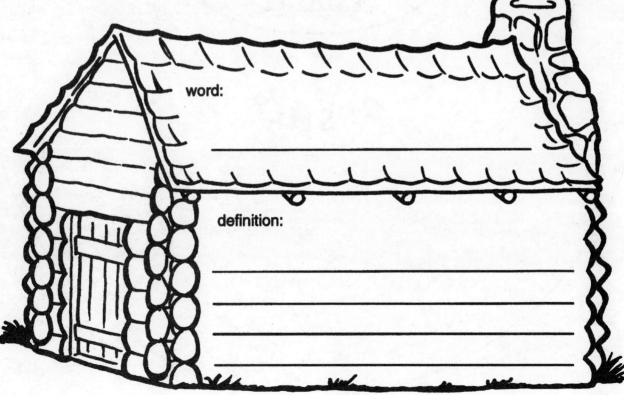

word:

_____

definition:

_____

_____

_____

Roanoke Island Q & A Datadisk

1. Glue the disk onto a piece of oaktag and cut out the perimeter of the datadisk.
2. Use the datadisk as a template to cut a circle out of the second piece of oaktag.
3. Cut out the Q and A spaces on the first disk.
4. Place the Q and A datadisk over the blank circle and fasten them together with a brad pushed through the center dot.
5. Fill out the "Roanoke Island" word web according to your teacher's directions.
6. Write a title for the datadisk using creative lettering, and draw a related illustration.
7. Write your questions in the "Question" space and your answers in the "Answer" space, rotating the datadisk each time.

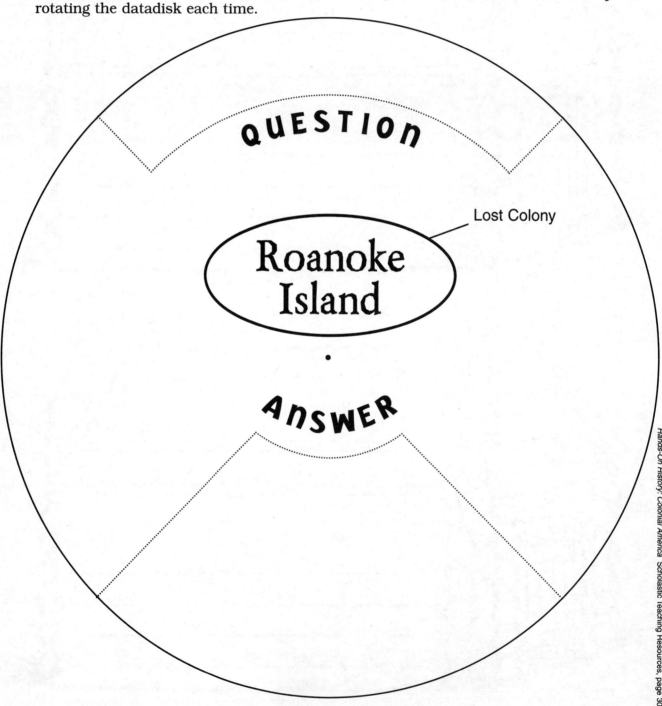

QUESTION

Lost Colony

Roanoke Island

ANSWER

Jamestown Study Guide

WORD BANK: Use the words and phrases below to fill in the blanks. Each answer will be used only once.

Africans	John Smith	Powhatan	tobacco
died	food	gold	women
House of Burgesses	mosquitoes	The Starving Time	
Indians	new settlers	swampy land	

(Fold this tab back and tape it to the brainstorming web page.)

Reasons Why Jamestown Grew and Prospered:

- _____ helped provide food and supplies.

- _____'s strong leadership helped.

- _____ became the cash crop.

- _____ arrived to join the men of the colony.

- _____ were brought and forced to work without pay.

- Free land was given to _____.

- The _____ was formed, giving colonists a say in government.

Problems the Colonists Faced:

- Jamestown was located on _____.

- Colonists were lazy and only wanted to search for _____.

- They ran out of _____. (This period was known as _____.)

- More than half of the colonists _____ the first winter.

- They were plagued by disease-carrying _____.

- The colonists had fights with the _____.

(Fold this tab back and tape it to the brainstorming web page.)

Comparing the Colonies

NAME: _____ DATE: _____

Compare the three English colonies by writing the correct code letter in the answer column next to each phrase. Some phrases may have more than one correct answer. As you correct the answers in class, write a check in the correcting column if your answer is correct. If it is wrong, write an X over your answer and write the correct answer in the correcting column.

KEY: R = Roanoke   J = Jamestown   P = Plymouth

SCORE

Answer Column	Correcting Column	
_____	_____	1. Founded for religious freedom.
_____	_____	2. Founded to make money for the Virginia Company of London.
_____	_____	3. The "Lost Colony."
_____	_____	4. Tobacco helped it succeed.
_____	_____	5. The first English child in America was born here.
_____	_____	6. Site of the first Thanksgiving.
_____	_____	7. Pocahontas helped this colony.
_____	_____	8. The *Mayflower* landed here.
_____	_____	9. John Smith settled here.
_____	_____	10. Many colonists here died.
_____	_____	11. The only clue was "Croatoan."
_____	_____	12. Located off the coast of present-day North Carolina.
_____	_____	13. Located in present-day Massachusetts.
_____	_____	14. Located in present-day Virginia.
_____	_____	15. Located on swampy land.
_____	_____	16. This colony eventually prospered.
_____	_____	17. The House of Burgesses began here.
_____	_____	18. The Mayflower Compact was the law here.
_____	_____	19. Squanto helped the colonists here.
_____	_____	20. Founded by Sir Walter Raleigh.

Map of the Thirteen Colonies

NAME: _____ DATE: _____

As you learn about the thirteen colonies, add information to the map below. First, color code each of the boxes in the key. Then, as you learn about each colony, list it under the correct heading, color in the colony on the map, and label it with the postal abbreviation of the current state.

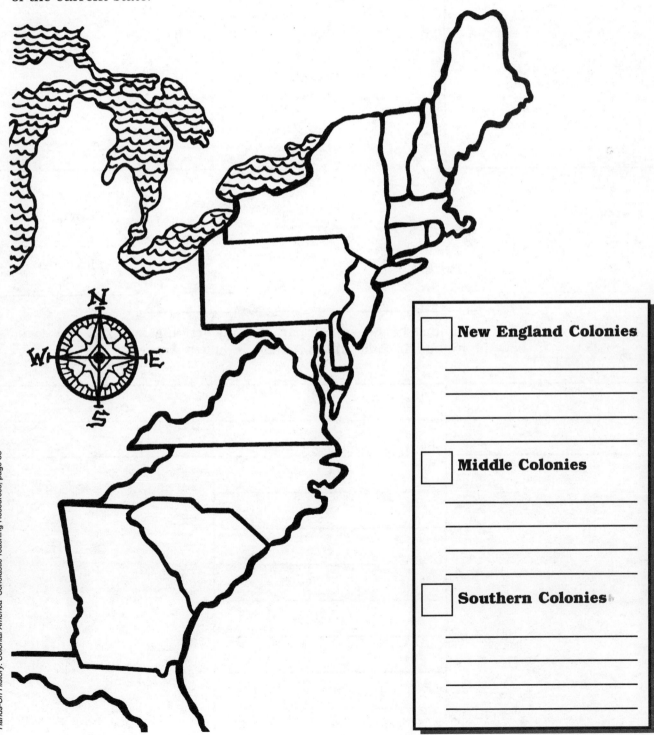

☐ **New England Colonies**

_____

_____

_____

☐ **Middle Colonies**

_____

_____

_____

☐ **Southern Colonies**

_____

_____

_____

Four-Fold Book of the New England Colonies

Triangular Trade Four-Fold Book

Dropped Off _____

Picked Up _____

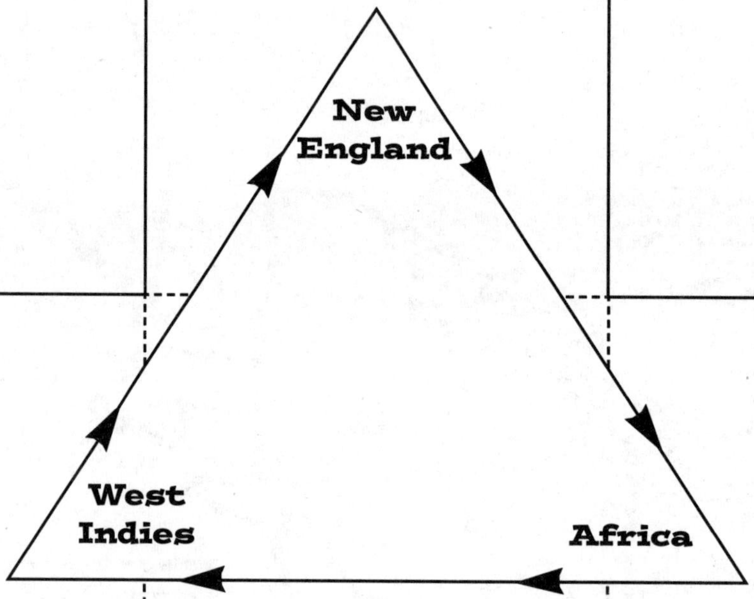

New England

Dropped Off

_____

Picked Up

_____

West Indies

Africa

Dropped Off

_____

Picked Up

_____

On the lines below, write a paragraph describing
how the triangular trade got its name and how it worked.

_____

_____

_____

_____

_____

_____

_____

_____

_____

Matchbooks of the Southern Colonies

Virginia	Maryland	North and South Carolina

Georgia

Slaves and Indentured Servants

NAME: _____ DATE: _____

First, complete the key by color-coding the boxes: blue for slaves, yellow for indentured servants, green for both. Then fill in the boxes in the answer column next to each phrase. As you correct the answers in class, write a check in the correcting column if your answer is correct. If it is wrong, write an X over your answer and put the correct color in the correcting column.

KEY

☐ = INDENTURED SERVANTS
☐ = SLAVES
☐ = BOTH

SCORE

Answer Column   *Correcting Column*

1. They chose to work in America.
2. They were both men and women.
3. They usually came from England.
4. Their children became servants.
5. The majority of them were white.
6. These servants were black.
7. They worked without pay.
8. They agreed to work for five to seven years, and then were freed.
9. Most of them came from Africa.
10. The master provided food, clothing, and shelter.
11. They were forced to work.
12. They were bought and sold like property.
13. They agreed to work in exchange for passage to America.
14. Many died on the voyage to America.
15. They worked until they died or were set free.
16. They could not get a new job without permission.

Worlds Apart

NAME: _____ DATE: _____

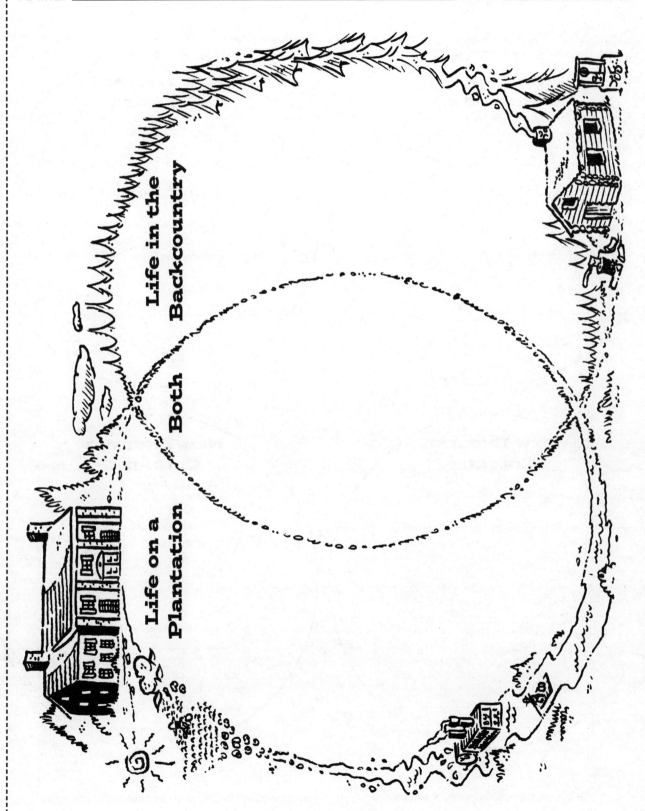

Life in the Backcountry

Both

Life on a Plantation

Circlebook: The New England Colonies

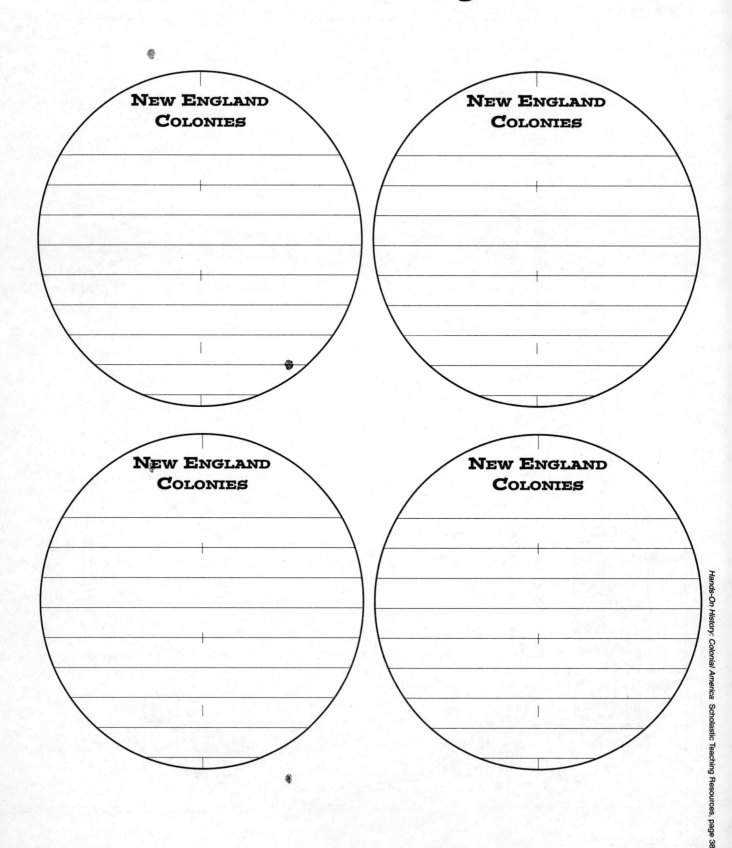

NEW ENGLAND
COLONIES

NEW ENGLAND
COLONIES

NEW ENGLAND
COLONIES

NEW ENGLAND
COLONIES

Circlebook: The Middle Colonies

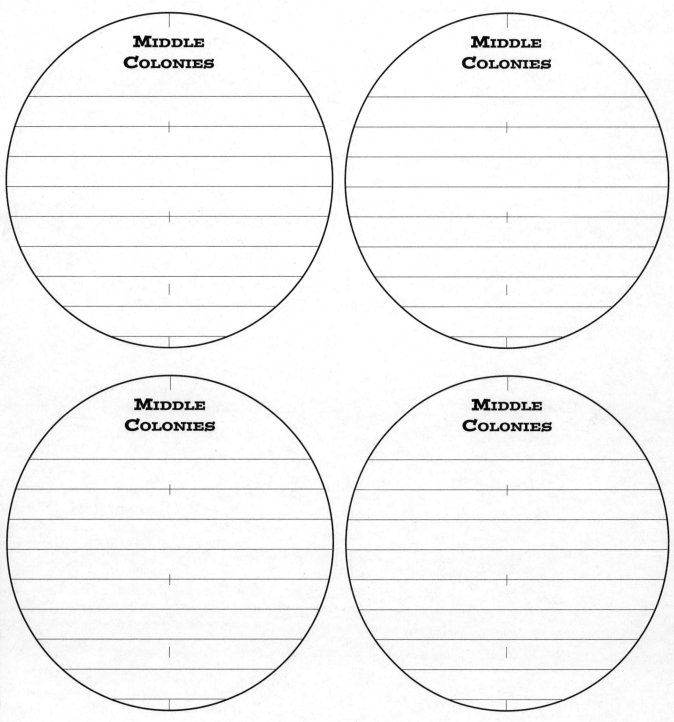

Circlebook: The Southern Colonies

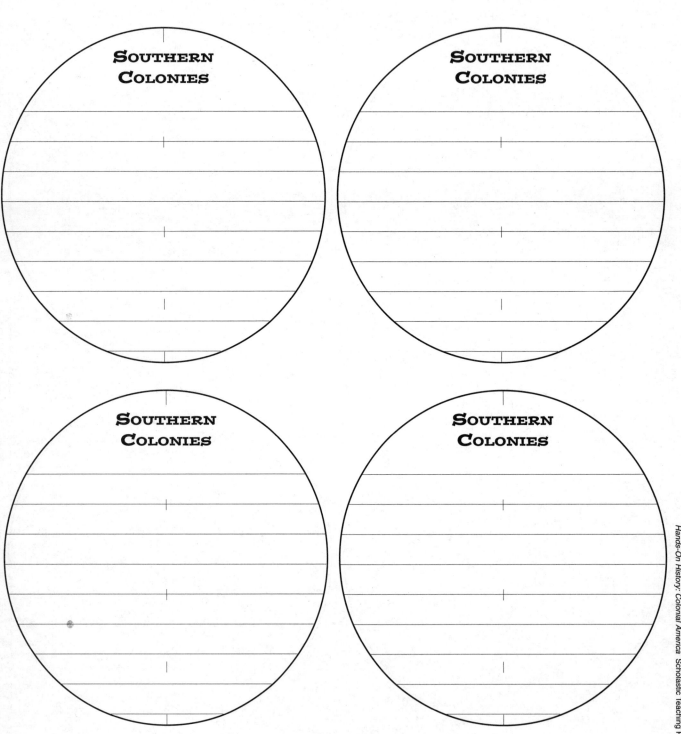

SOUTHERN COLONIES

SOUTHERN COLONIES

SOUTHERN COLONIES

SOUTHERN COLONIES

Colonial Quilt Template

1. Use creative lettering to write the name of your topic in the square at the center of the template.
2. In the other eight sections, draw pictures or designs that relate to your research topic. Make your designs in repeating or alternating patterns, similar to an actual quilt square.
3. Cut out your quilt panel and wait for your teacher's instructions.

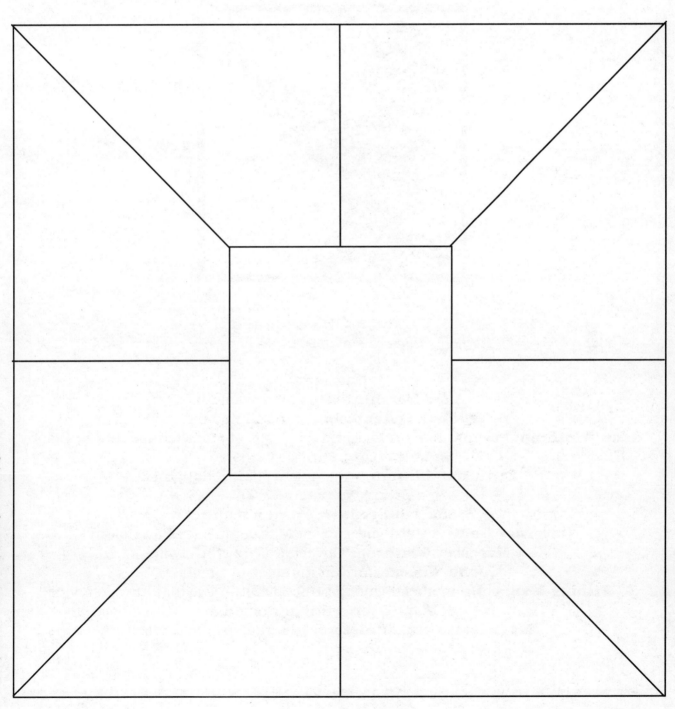

Anne Hutchinson: An Outspoken Woman

by Sarah J. Glasscock

Cast of Characters
(in order of appearance)

Narrator
Anne Hutchinson: Puritan woman
William Hutchinson: Anne's husband
John Winthrop: Puritan man and second governor of Massachusetts Bay Colony
John Cotton: Puritan minister
Faith Hutchinson: Anne and William's daughter
Young Women 1 & 2
Zachariah Symmes: Puritan minister
Governor Dudley: third governor of Massachusetts Bay Colony
Margaret Winthrop: Governor Winthrop's wife
John Wilson: Puritan minister in Boston
Tithing Man: church official who kept people from leaving during service
Mary Dyer: Puritan woman
Magistrates and Ministers 1–4 (nonspeaking roles)

Hands-On History: Colonial America Scholastic Teaching Resources, page 42

Act 1

Scene 1: April 8, 1630. Southampton, England.

NARRATOR: In the 1600s, England had an official church—the Church of England. Its leader was the King of England. Anyone who disagreed with the teachings of the church was also going against the king. It was dangerous—and illegal—to disagree with the king. The Puritans, however, believed that the Church of England needed to be changed. Some Puritans decided to sail to America to set up a new community where they would be free to worship as they chose.

ANNE HUTCHINSON: Reverend Cotton, your sermons are always so clear. You answer all my questions and put my mind at rest. I think everyone sailing to America will miss your sermons.

WILLIAM HUTCHINSON: I'm certainly glad you're staying here in England, Cotton. If not, Anne would have us packed up and ready to board the *Griffin*, too.

JOHN WINTHROP: We'll miss the Reverend Cotton, Mrs. Hutchinson, but we have many good ministers traveling with us. Think of it! A whole community of Puritans! We'll be free to worship as we choose. We'll be free to speak our minds. Reverend Cotton, your life is in danger here because you speak the truth. You would do well to join us.

JOHN COTTON: I wish you and the others the best of luck, Mr. Winthrop. But my place is here, where there's so little freedom and so much fear.

ANNE HUTCHINSON: Our numbers are growing. The King will surely allow the changes we demand in the church.

JOHN WINTHROP: Don't be so sure, Mrs. Hutchinson. We say that the Bible is more important than the leaders of the church. The King doesn't want to give up any power.

ANNE HUTCHINSON: Not many men want to give up power. As for women—we have none to give up.

JOHN WINTHROP: You carry more power than you imagine, Mrs. Hutchinson. Your words are strong.

ANNE HUTCHINSON: I speak my mind, Mr. Winthrop. As a Puritan, that is only right.

JOHN WINTHROP: It's always wise to think before you speak.

WILLIAM HUTCHINSON: Set your mind at rest, Mr. Winthrop. A great deal of thought goes into Anne's words. *(shaking hands with John Winthrop)* Good luck!

(The Hutchinsons leave.)

JOHN COTTON: It's true. Mrs. Hutchinson does think a great deal.

JOHN WINTHROP: She would do well to listen a great deal, too.

Scene 2: Summer, 1634. On the deck of the *Griffin* as it makes another trip to America.

NARRATOR: From his pulpit, John Cotton continued to demand changes in the Church of England. In 1632, with their lives in danger, the reverend and his wife had to flee to America. After much thought, Anne Hutchinson and her family followed Reverend Cotton to the Massachusetts Bay Colony, which John Winthrop and the Puritans had founded in New England. On the trip, Reverend Zachariah Symmes held church services for the passengers.

ANNE HUTCHINSON: Give me your needle, Faith, and I'll thread it for you.

FAITH HUTCHINSON: The ship rolls so, I can't keep my hands still. How much longer do you think we'll be at sea?

ANNE HUTCHINSON: What would you say if I told you we should reach New England in three weeks?

FAITH HUTCHINSON: I'd say that's not soon enough, Mother.

YOUNG WOMAN 1: Excuse me, Mrs. Hutchinson? I don't mean to disturb you.

ANNE HUTCHINSON: You cause us no disturbance. Please, sit down. How may I help you?

YOUNG WOMAN 1: I—we . . . well, we couldn't help but notice that you walked out of Reverend Symmes' service this morning.

YOUNG WOMAN 2: In the middle of his sermon!

ANNE HUTCHINSON: I disagree with his teachings.

YOUNG WOMAN 2: But he's a minister! Shouldn't he know what he's talking about?

ANNE HUTCHINSON: Yes, he should.

YOUNG WOMAN 1: I don't really see how you can disagree with him . . .

FAITH HUTCHINSON: You don't know my mother.

ANNE HUTCHINSON: Puritan teachings are very clear. Success in business and wealth are not signs of God's approval. Reverend Symmes seemed to say this morning that having a fine house and property will get you into heaven. But only God chooses those He will save.

YOUNG WOMAN 2: I pray every day and obey the commandments. I help others . . .

YOUNG WOMAN 1: Then it is what is inside you, rather than the things you do or surround yourself with, that earns God's favor?

ANNE HUTCHINSON: Exactly!

(Reverend Zachariah Symmes approaches the group.)

ZACHARIAH SYMMES: Mrs. Hutchinson, I trust you are well? I noted that you left in the middle of my sermon.

ANNE HUTCHINSON: I'm quite well, thank you.

ZACHARIAH SYMMES: Ah, then you do not find the word of God to be wholesome?

ANNE HUTCHINSON: The word of God is indeed wholesome, Reverend, but your words trouble me.

ZACHARIAH SYMMES: I beg your pardon? Perhaps if you'd stayed to hear all of my sermon . . .

ANNE HUTCHINSON: I don't think so. Did you not say that doing good deeds is a sign of God's approval? Anyone can do a good deed. What does that prove?

ZACHARIAH SYMMES: (*growing angry*) Ministers preach the word of God. Ordinary men do not. Ordinary women definitely do not.

ANNE HUTCHINSON: When we reach Boston, Reverend Symmes, listen to Reverend Cotton. You'll see that there is something beyond the words you preach. I have many things to say to you, but I fear that you cannot bear them now.

(Reverend Symmes stalks off.)

YOUNG WOMAN 1: You used such strong words with Reverend Symmes . . .

YOUNG WOMAN 2: Did you see how red his face got? I've never seen him so angry.

ANNE HUTCHINSON: He is a minister. He should preach our beliefs correctly.

Act 2

Scene 1: Autumn, 1634. Massachusetts Bay Colony. Inside Governor Dudley's house.

NARRATOR: Reverend Symmes didn't forget—or forgive—Anne Hutchinson. All newcomers to the Massachusetts Bay Colony had to apply to join the Puritan church there. Both Anne and William Hutchinson applied. Each met with the church leaders and answered their questions. William was accepted immediately into the church. Weeks passed, and Anne received no word. Then one day she was called to the Governor's house.

GOVERNOR DUDLEY: Thank you for coming, Mrs. Hutchinson. I believe you already know Reverend Cotton, Reverend Symmes, and Reverend Wilson? They have more questions for you.

ANNE HUTCHINSON: I know Reverend Cotton well, and Reverend Wilson less well. Reverend Symmes is no stranger to me.

ZACHARIAH SYMMES: Let's begin. Didn't you say you could predict the future when we were on board the *Griffin*?

ANNE HUTCHINSON: I did not. You might as well say that I am a witch.

ZACHARIAH SYMMES: I heard you tell your daughter that we would be in New England in three weeks.

ANNE HUTCHINSON: I did say that, but . . .

ZACHARIAH SYMMES: And didn't it come true?

ANNE HUTCHINSON: Yes, we reached Boston Harbor in three weeks . . .

ZACHARIAH SYMMES: Didn't you argue with me on board the ship? Didn't you tell me that what I was preaching was wrong? Tell us all how useless good deeds are.

ANNE HUTCHINSON: Reverend Cotton, I only tried to explain our Puritan beliefs as you explain them so clearly in your sermons.

JOHN COTTON: I have said before, and say again, that ownership of a home and property, doing well in business and doing good deeds, are not signs of God's approval.

GOVERNOR DUDLEY: So Mrs. Hutchinson was repeating your words, Reverend Cotton?

JOHN COTTON: Yes, she was.

GOVERNOR DUDLEY: Then I see no problem. Mrs. Hutchinson, welcome to the church.

Scene 2: 1635. Massachusetts Bay Colony. Inside John and Margaret Winthrop's house.

NARRATOR: Although she became a church member, Anne Hutchinson still wasn't fully accepted within the Puritan community. Many women met during the week to discuss the ministers' sermons and other religious matters. Anne Hutchinson hadn't gone to any of these meetings because she didn't think the talk was always serious enough. People began to say that she was too proud. To overcome their criticism, Anne Hutchinson started leading her own meetings.

JOHN WINTHROP: Where are you going, Margaret?

MARGARET WINTHROP: Across the street to the Hutchinsons' house. It's the Tuesday meeting. I always go, you know that.

JOHN WINTHROP: What goes on in those meetings? It seems that more and more people attend each week.

MARGARET WINTHROP: Anne usually talks about Reverend Cotton's sermons. She answers questions about what he said. He's sometimes hard to understand.

JOHN WINTHROP: If they have questions, they would do better to ask Reverend Cotton himself, or another minister.

MARGARET WINTHROP: But aren't we here in America so we can hold meetings and discuss things? We wouldn't be able to do this in England. We've been holding meetings since we first arrived.

JOHN WINTHROP: Not everyone is as outspoken as Mrs. Hutchinson is. She claims to know too much. A woman like that can be very dangerous, putting ideas into people's minds.

MARGARET WINTHROP: She's able to explain things very clearly to people. If she worries you so, John, then come with me. See for yourself what goes on.

JOHN WINTHROP: No, thank you. I don't need Mrs. Hutchinson to explain anything to me.

Act 3

Scene 1: Fall, 1636. Inside the Puritan church in Boston.

NARRATOR: The Massachusetts Bay Colony was now divided. On one side were Anne Hutchinson and her followers, called Antinomians, or people who are against law. On the other side were John Winthrop and most of the ministers. The Reverend John Wheelwright, Anne's brother-in-law, arrived in Boston. The Antinomians wanted him to preach alongside John Cotton in the Boston church. John Winthrop voted against Wheelwright. Since everyone had to agree on important church decisions, Anne Hutchinson and her followers lost. They showed their disappointment by walking out of church one day.

JOHN WILSON: I have a few announcements before I begin my sermon today. John Winthrop has asked me to say that the General Court will meet tomorrow afternoon at two o'clock.

(Anne Hutchinson gets up from her seat and goes to the back of the church.)

ANNE HUTCHINSON: Excuse me, sir, but I don't feel well. I must leave.

TITHING MAN: You don't look ill to me, Mrs. Hutchinson. Why don't you take a few deep breaths and return to your seat?

ANNE HUTCHINSON: No, sir, I must leave now.

TITHING MAN: Very well. You may go out.

(Mary Dyer and other women begin coming to the back of the church, too.)

MARY DYER: My child is feverish. I must take her home.

TITHING MAN: What's going on here? What are you up to?

MARY DYER: Feel her forehead. See for yourself how hot it is.

TITHING MAN: Go on then. Be quick about it.

YOUNG WOMAN 1: Leave the door open, sir. I must go, too. My little John is colicky. I don't want him to disturb Reverend Wilson's sermon.

TITHING MAN: But he's sleeping! He's not . . .

YOUNG WOMAN 1: I'm his mother, aren't I? Do you want me to tell Reverend Wilson why little John cried all during his sermon?

TITHING MAN: Out with you then. Be quick! Be quick!

YOUNG WOMAN 2: An emergency, sir. I'm sure I left my broom too close to the fire. My house will surely burn down if I don't leave right now.

TITHING MAN: Now, just a minute here!

(John Winthrop hurries to the back of the church.)

JOHN WINTHROP: What's going on here? Why are you letting all these women leave?

TITHING MAN: They're ill—or their children are—or they've got to tend to an emergency.

JOHN WINTHROP: Anne Hutchinson is behind this, I know she is. Mark my words: This time she's gone too far.

Scene 2: November, 1637. Inside the Newtown Puritan church.

NARRATOR: In the summer of 1637, 25 Puritan leaders held a synod, or meeting. They spelled out a list of 82 errors in the way the Puritan community was thinking. Most of the errors pointed to things Anne Hutchinson and her followers said and did. The Antinomians ignored the list. Governor Winthrop and his followers decided that something stronger had to be done. They put Anne Hutchinson on trial.

JOHN WINTHROP: Mrs. Hutchinson, you are called here as one of those that have troubled the peace of this colony and the churches here. You are known to be a woman who has a great share in causing this trouble. You've insulted our churches and their ministers. You've continued to hold meetings in your house, even though the synod outlawed them. You must obey the decision of this court or you'll be banished from the colony.

ANNE HUTCHINSON: I am called here to answer before you, but I hear no things said against me. What have I said or done? I have never harmed my church or community.

JOHN WINTHROP: As I said before, the synod outlawed your meetings, yet you continued to hold them. You must not do anything that goes against the authorities of this colony. You must not encourage others to do so.

ANNE HUTCHINSON: If you have a rule for it from God's word, then please show it to me. I have brought my Bible.

JOHN WINTHROP: You show me where it says in the Bible that women may hold meetings and preach the word of God. Is Mrs. Hutchinson guilty or innocent? Let me see a show of hands. Guilty? (All the magistrates and ministers raise their hands, including Winthrop.) Innocent? (No one raises a hand.) Mrs. Hutchinson, it has been decided. You are not fit for our society. You are hereby banished from the Massachusetts Bay Colony.

ANNE HUTCHINSON: I have done nothing wrong. I have only spoken out to help my church and community. That is why we Puritans came here. Have we forgotten that so soon?

NARRATOR: Anne Hutchinson and her family left the colony and moved to Portsmouth, Rhode Island. William Hutchinson died four years later. The family then went to New York. Sadly, Anne Hutchinson and most of her ch̶i̶l̶d̶r̶e̶n̶ ̶w̶e̶r̶e̶ ̶k̶i̶l̶l̶e̶d̶ ̶i̶n̶ ̶a̶n̶ ̶a̶t̶t̶a̶c̶k̶ in 1643.